Written by Bethany Latham

Like Yours, Like Mine

HAIR

KidHaven PUBLISHING

Published in 2027 by
KidHaven Publishing, an Imprint of Greenhaven Publishing, LLC
2544 Clinton St., Buffalo, NY 14224

Written by: Bethany Latham
Edited by: Rebecca Phillips-Bartlett
Designed by: Ian McMullen

Cataloging-in-Publication Data
Names: Latham, Bethany.
Title: Hair / Bethany Latham.
Description: Buffalo, NY : KidHaven Publishing, 2027. | Series: Like yours, like mine | Includes glossary and index.
Identifiers: ISBN 9781534570917 (pbk.) | ISBN 9781534570924 (library bound) | ISBN 9781534570931 (ebook)
Subjects: LCSH: Hair--Juvenile literature.
Classification: LCC QP88.3 L384 2027 | DDC 573.58--dc23

Printed in the United States

CPSIA compliance information: Batch #CS27KH: For further information contact Greenhaven Publishing LLC at 1-844-317-7404.

Please visit our website, www.greenhavenpublishing.com.
For a free color catalog of all our high-quality books, call toll free 1-844-317-7404 or fax 1-844-317-7405.

Find us on

IMAGE CREDITS
Images courtesy of Shutterstock.com, unless otherwise stated.
Cover - Ground Picture, Roman Samborskyi, K-FK
4-5 - Monkey Business Images, Anatoliy Karlyuk. 6-7 - Sakura Image Inc, Roman Samborskyi, Krakenimages.com, ShotPrime Studio. 8-9 - Rawpixel.com, AYO Production, New Africa. 10-11 - Kiselev Andrey Valerevich, Mr.Cheangchai Noojuntuk, Master of Stocks, Asier Romero. 12-13 - Pixel-Shot, Jacob Lund, Brester Irina. 14-15 - CarlosDavid, Ana Rosa D. Ribeiro, Andrey Arkusha, Adeteye Adeniyi. 16-17 - Josep Suria, Vadiar, Nelson Antoine, ViDI Studio. 18-19 - Jose y yo Estudio, Khosro, Kues, vhpicstock, Ivan_Shenets, Roman Samborskyi. 20-21 - Sebastian Vergara, SibRapid, valeraa_valeraa. 22-23 - DiversityStudio, PeopleImages.

CONTENTS

Words that look like **THIS** can be found in the glossary on page 24.

WE'RE ALL DIFFERENT

There are billions of people living on our planet. It is a busy place! And do you know the most amazing part? No two people are exactly the same. Everybody is **UNIQUE**.

Our bodies are **DIVERSE** and amazing things. People can choose to make them even more unique through personal style. Hairstyles can be a wonderful way to show the world who you are.

Let's explore the wonderful world of human hair!

HAIR TYPES

Human hair is an amazing thing. There are so many ways it can grow. There are four main hair types. They are based on how curly the hair is. The four hair types are...

Hair type is a **SPECTRUM**. A person's hair type can also change over the course of their life.

Each hair type needs to be cared for differently, such as by using different hair products.

COLOR

The four main **NATURAL** hair colors are red, black, blonde and brown.

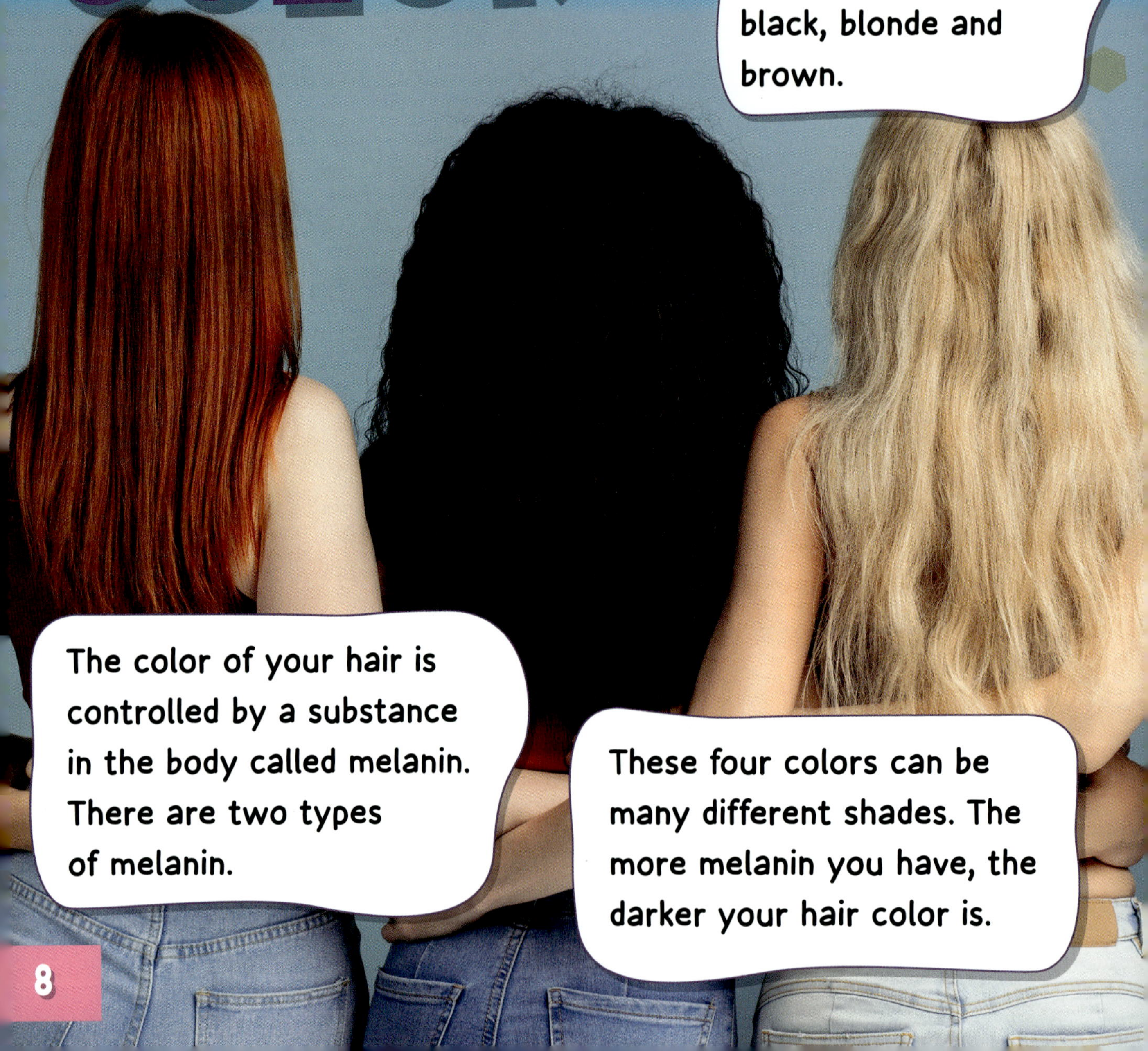

The color of your hair is controlled by a substance in the body called melanin. There are two types of melanin.

These four colors can be many different shades. The more melanin you have, the darker your hair color is.

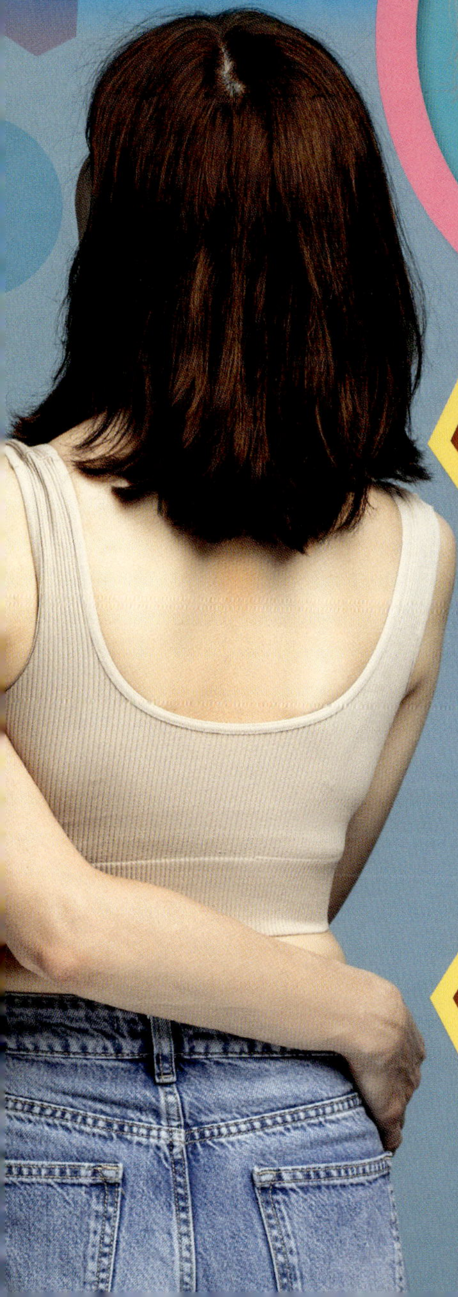

Some people dye their hair bright colors. Hair dye is a way for people to express their personalities!

Dyeing hair should always be done safely and carefully.

As people get older, their hair can turn white or gray.

LENGTH

There are so many different lengths hair can be. People can wear it short, or they can choose to grow it out. Usually, people wear their hair at a length that is comfortable for them.

Some people's hair can grow very long. Other people's hair can only grow to a certain point. This is because of **GENETICS**. People's genetics control their hair length and how fast it grows.

Some people have no hair or lose hair over time. Having no hair is known as being bald. Some people might choose to shave their head. For some people, a medical condition might mean they lose or cannot grow their hair.

A condition called alopecia and some medical treatments can cause hair loss. Sometimes, the person's hair might grow back over time. Other times, the hair loss lasts forever.

Some people choose to shave their heads.

HAIRSTYLES

Hairstyles are a great way for people to show the world who they are. Hairstyles can be as diverse as the people who wear them. They can be practical or decorative. Sometimes, they are both!

People may use their hairstyles to show they are part of a certain group. Some **CULTURES** have hairstyles that are important to them. Fans of punk music might choose to have punk hairstyles.

Punk Hairstyle

A hairstyle from the Bantu culture

HAIR COVERINGS

Many people around the world choose to cover their hair. This is often done for religious reasons. Some Muslim women choose to wear headscarves, such as hijabs. Some Jewish men wear yarmulkes.

Some Christian women choose to wear headscarves. Many Sikh people choose to wear a dastar, or turban. These head coverings are all ways of showing someone's faith.

FACIAL HAIR

There are many different styles of facial hair. They can look just as varied as the hairstyles on people's heads! Do you know anyone who has a beard or a mustache?

Just like the hair on top of our heads, beards can grow very long. Some people choose to braid them or decorate them with beads. Other people style their facial hair into amazing shapes using wax.

Some people hold competitions to judge the fanciest beard!

BODY HAIR

Hair does not just grow on the head and face. It grows all over our bodies too. Anyone can have body hair in lots of different places. These include the arms, legs, chest, and armpits.

Some people may have more body hair than others. It is all due to genetics. Some people choose to shave their body hair. Others let it grow. All body hair is natural and normal!

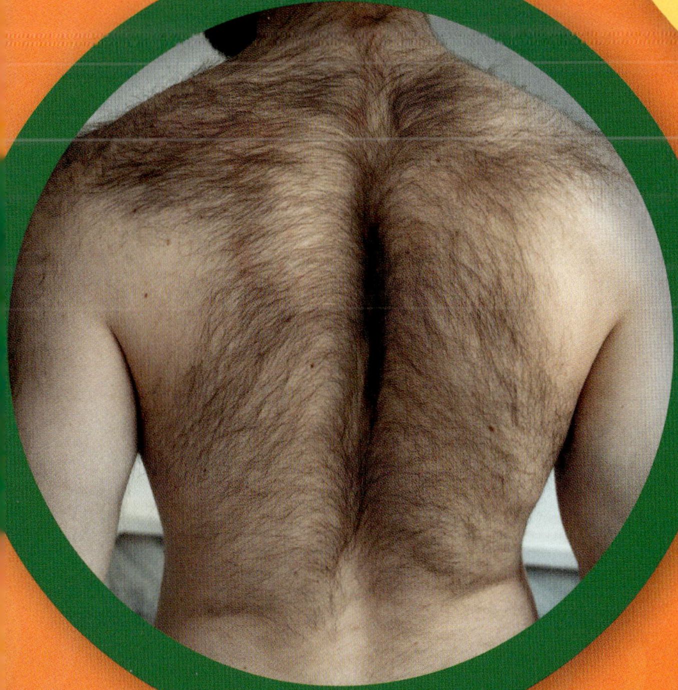

Body hair can be a different color than the hair on your head.

WHAT ABOUT YOUR HAIR?

Hair is beautiful and diverse. There are so many different types, colors, and styles. Whether someone has a lot of hair or a little, it is part of what makes them unique.

What about your hair? What color is it? How do you like to style it? What do you think your hair says about you? Remember, your hair is wonderful, just like you are!

GLOSSARY

cultures
the traditions, ideas, and ways of life of groups of people

diverse
a way of describing a group of varied and different things

genetics to do with genes, which are the instructions that tell the body how to work

natural
found in nature and not made by people

spectrum
a scale or wide range of things

unique
unlike anything or anyone else

INDEX